# Home for Christmas Youth Study Book

**Home for Christmas:**
**Tales of Hope and Second Chances**
**Youth Study Book**

***Home for Christmas***
978-1-5018-7044-6
978-1-5018-7045-3 *eBook*

***Home for Christmas: DVD***
978-1-5018-7048-4

***Home for Christmas: Leader Guide***
978-1-5018-7046-0
978-1-5018-7047-7 *eBook*

***Home for Christmas: Youth Study Book***
978-1-5018-7042-2
978-1-5018-7043-9 *eBook*

YOUTH STUDY BOOK BY ANTHONY PETERSON

Abingdon Press / Nashville

**Home for Christmas**
Tales of Hope and Second Chances
Youth Study Book



978-1-5018-7042-2



18 19 20 21 22 23 24 25 26 27 — 10 9 8 7 6 5 4 3 2 1
MANUFACTURED IN THE UNITED STATES OF AMERICA

# Contents

# INTRODUCTION

The idea of home really moves me. When I think of heaven, my favorite association is home.

I love home so much I made a playlist all about the idea of "home." The playlist includes pop, rock, hip-hop, gospel, and country songs, and not a little bit of old school R&B. To prepare my playlist, I conducted a search on a music streaming service. From my search of "home" almost half of the songs were holiday songs.

During the holiday season, we see lots of ads, movies, and, well, songs about home. For Christians the holiday anticipation found in Advent is a perfect time to be reminded of the home in God we are always invited to return to. It's a time of hope and expectation, of joy and thanksgiving for the home we're offered, the home we see in the birth of Jesus.

In the family I grew up in, our house changed from year to year. The building was not our home; our home was wherever our family was. And while my family life was not perfect, our home was safe and loving.

Of course, not everyone has a home that feels that way. Not everyone has a house to come home to. Across the U.S. and beyond, people are missing homes. Some live in shelters that can barely be called home. Some shelters are not safe, not warm, not home. Some of the residents feel safer on the streets.

Other folks are in families that are nothing like the loving, safe one I grew up in. Poverty may mean no food, no heat in the winter, or no air conditioning in the summer. There is neglect and abuse, and sometimes a simple lack of love.

And some go looking for that "home" or that "family" in other places. In East Los Angeles, one place to look for family is in gangs. Those gangs can provide a purpose and a sense of community or family. But that purpose and family come at a big price. Gang violence leads to incarceration and death for people who were only seeking a home.

Thirty years ago Father Greg Boyle, or "G-Dog," "Father G," or simply "G," began spending time with some of these gangbangers. Over the years his relationships have grown into the largest gang-intervention and post-lockup rehabilitation and reentry program in the world. Young people who have had enough of gangs or who have just gotten out of incarceration are finding a safe, loving home with Homeboy Industries.

What Father G saw in those early days was something he called "a lethal absence of hope." He found ways to create hope by helping them survive and thrive. Through the years Father G and Homeboy Industries have offered services such as tattoo removal, education, anger-management and substance abuse classes, counseling, legal help, and job training. Homeboys and homegirls get job training through businesses like silk screening, the Homeboy Bakery, and the Homegirl Cafe.

And on top of everything, they find a home, where they come together in celebration, support, and kinship. For many of them, Homeboy is the first home they have ever had. For others, it is the only safe home they have ever had.

This Advent study is looking at Homeboy Industries as a place that's changing things for people without a home, a family, or a friendly or safe place to be in this world. Homeboy works each year with more than 8,000 individuals who are looking for hope and second chances. In this Advent study we will hear some of their stories.

The holiday season is a time when many people feel the loneliness and homelessness the most. People who live in situations of violence and poverty often can't think of the holiday season the way the rest of us do. But because homeboys and homegirls have found hope, love, joy, and peace with Homeboy Industries, this is a great time to learn from their experience as we await the promises of Advent, especially the arrival of Jesus Christ.

# USING THIS BOOK

This study is made up of four sessions:

1. A Home for Hope
2. A Home for Love
3. A Home for Joy
4. A Home for Peace

## *Introduction*

Every session begins with an introduction of the weekly topic, based on the Advent calendar.

A variety of activities follows, including:

## *Morning Meeting*

A day at Homeboy begins with a morning meeting. Everyone in the building gathers in the central lobby and around the balcony and stairs. The area has the feel of an intimate home, and the meeting itself is like a family gathering. During this time the "family" celebrates birthdays, the end of probation periods, and other milestones. At each morning meeting, someone offers the thought for the day.

In this study, each weekly session begins with a "Morning Meeting" devotional, which can be read by a leader or another participant.

## *Learning Activities*

Every session provides a variety of learning activities. Most of these activities can be done using almost any size group with a minimum number of materials.

## Week 1

# A Home for Hope

I would hate to be an electronic device. Because it happens every few months: a new phone is introduced; or a new tablet, laptop, or desktop computer. Some folks are fortunate enough and eager enough to buy the new device immediately. They have heard about it, read about it, and anticipated the release date. They buy the new one and either put away, give away, sell away, throw away, or otherwise dispose of the older gadget. The older gadget probably works perfectly well, but times have changed, and the new is thought to always be better.

So what happens to that older device? If it was sold or given away, it might get life for another year or two. Those of us who aren't fortunate enough or eager enough will happily or unhappily buy last year's model. We are content that it is better than the one we currently own. But in time that older device that is new to us is put away, given away, sold away, thrown away, or otherwise disposed of again. Even if we wanted to keep it, the issuing company won't support it, almost makes you feel embarrassed for still having it.

Eventually throwing away is the only option. And in most communities, that means the device will end up in a landfill, serving no one, and actually harming the environment. Tons of electronic waste, or e-waste, are heaping up in our landfills.

But some companies are finding ways to recycle those devices. Homeboy Recycling is one of those companies. As Kabira Stokes, CEO of Homeboy Recycling, puts it, "Here in California, we have two huge problems—our landfills are overflowing; our prisons are overflowing. We believe we can solve both these problems at the same time through green job reentry training programs." She says, "Seven out of ten people who leave a California correctional facility return within three years. It's not because they enjoyed their stay there. It's because it is a broken system."[1]

And for her, the beauty of training previously incarcerated people to recycle electronics is that it reminds us that both the workers and the old devices still have value. It's a message that we easily miss in a disposable world. Our prisons and jails can easily be treated as places to dispose of unwanted people, people treated much the same way we treat old electronics.

It is too easy to think of people who have committed crimes as people we can throw away. But that is not what the Christian story says. According to the Christian story, no one reaches the point of being worthless. Each of us is valuable to a loving God, no matter what. The story of the Lost Son in the Bible is a great illustration.

A young man tells his father that he is leaving home and he wants the inheritance due to him. He basically says, "Dad, I can't wait for you to die. I want to get whatever is coming to me now." Rather than argue with him, the father grants his request. The young man leaves home, goes to another country, and spends all of the money on all of the worst things. He is finally out of money and ends up trying to find work. He finds himself feeding food to pigs and hoping to eat the food they eat. He is poor, depressed, lonely,

1 "The Story and Mission of Homeboy Recycling (Formerly Isidore Electronics Recycling)," Homeboy Recycling channel, YouTube, March 6, 2014, https://youtu.be/v9ozgGTeZ90.

and feeling guilty. And then he remembers home. He decides to hope maybe he can return. He remembers how loving his father was. He decides to take a chance on that love. He rehearses the words that he thinks might work: "Father, I have sinned against God and against you. Please take me home and treat me like one of your servants." He figures that's the best he deserves, and maybe the best his dad will give him. He travels back home, and as he's approaching the house, his father sees him. His father goes running out to him to welcome him home. The son can barely get his rehearsed speech out before his father starts planning a party for him! That's the kind of joy the father has in his son.

Father Greg Boyle, founder of Homeboy Industries, talks about God's love for all of us that way. He says that God delights in us—that God is too busy loving us to have any time left for disapproval. Like the lost son, we can confidently turn from anything and find a loving God ready to welcome us home. Though we are infinitely more valuable than old electronic devices, we can find new life just like they can. That is our hope.

## ACTIVITIES

Choose from the following activities to form your session.

### *Morning Meeting (5 minutes)*

Natalie doesn't tell us what she thinks about God. But she tells us what she once thought of herself. "When I first walked in the doors of Homeboys I don't think I could have looked at myself in the mirror. I couldn't even look at myself in the eyes because I didn't have no self-worth, no self-esteem."[2]

2 "Breaking the Cycle: Natalie's Story," Homeboy Industries channel, YouTube, December 13, 2017, https://youtu.be/l97M6oYhaZg.

When we are afraid to look at ourselves in the mirror, we're likely even more afraid to face the God of the universe. Many of us are accustomed to believing in a God who sees our every move, who knows our every thought, and who judges us for it all. Father G says, "The truth is, we're so used to... a one-false-move God."[3] This is the God who says, "I'm watching you and just waiting for you to mess up, so I can punish you." We've heard too many Christians condemn people—for their sexual orientation, for failed relationships, or for struggles with addiction.

Imagine that you're running in gangs, where you know criminal behavior is around you. Imagine that you can't see another, better life for yourself. Imagine that you can expect to be arrested or killed any day. What is the level of your hope? And especially if the God you know is the "One-false-move God"? We do not have to imagine, because if that is the nature of God, then we all—gangbangers and preachers and everyone else—are in the same boat.

But when Natalie walked into Homeboy, she found something else. It actually started when she was in prison. She received a letter from her son, who called her the best mom ever...while she was in prison. She says that that letter gave her hope.

Natalie is like the biblical Paul and Silas, who were arrested, beaten, and dragged off to prison. They had committed no crime and had every right to be bitter. But something in them gave them hope. And the night they were incarcerated, they started singing. Surely the songs only strengthened their hope. Surely they were thinking of another image of God. An image of God that reflects the hope Natalie was holding on to.

Father G says that we're not really accustomed to the "no matter whatness" of God. This is the idea that God loves us no matter what. "The 'no matter

3 Gregory Boyle, "The Calling of Delight: Gangs, Service, and Kinship," interview by Krista Tippett, *On Being*, The On Being Project, April 2, 2015, audio, 50:59, https://onbeing.org/programs/greg-boyle-the-calling-of-delight-gangs-service-and-kinship/.

whatness' of God dissolves the toxicity of shame and fills us with tender mercy."[4]

We don't know if Natalie was thinking about God in prison. But she did begin to find hope, a gift from the God who says, "I love you, no matter what." She felt that love because of a letter from her son, and it sustained her as a gift from God.

Natalie is now employed full-time with Homeboy Industries, offering hope to women like herself. She says, "Now when I look at myself in the mirror, I see myself as an educated homegirl, a Chicana, a mother, a strong woman. I just see Natalie. I just see a wonderful human being."

## *What If? (10 minutes)*

**Materials:** three pieces of paper for each participant, pens or pencils, three bowls

Give each student three pieces of paper. On the first piece of paper, have each student write a "What if..." question, such as "What if ice cream grew on trees?" or "What if your phone was made of chocolate?" On the second piece of paper have each student write a "then" statement, such as "then we would have cleaner streets" or "then clouds would rain popcorn."

Put all the "What if" questions in a bowl and all the "then" statements in another bowl. Pull one paper from each bowl and read them together.

After reading a few combinations, say, "Well, let's get serious. What if...Christmas was all that you want it to be? Advent is the time we spend waiting for Christmas. We learn this sense of anticipation early. Little children learn to anticipate gifts. But what about you? Besides gifts, what do you hope for in this season? Write down three hopes that you have for this season.

4 Gregory Boyle, *Tattoos on the Heart: The Power of Boundless Compassion* (New York: Free Press, 2010), 60.

Write three answers to the question 'What if Christmas was all that you want it to be?'"

Collect the papers and put them aside in a third bowl for later.

## *Tell Jennifer's Story (10 minutes)*

Read this passage from Justin Coleman's book *Home for Christmas*:

> It was the beginning of December, and Jennifer was incarcerated. Separated from her two small children, she spent Christmas facing the possibility of up to thirty-eight years in prison. After agreeing to a plea deal and arranging to live with her mother, Jennifer began working at Homeboy Industries. At first, everything was great; she and her children were making a new life together. But then her mother kicked the entire family out of the house. After such a promising start, Jennifer and her two children were homeless, and she felt like giving up and returning to her past life, and to the drugs and alcohol that had been part of it.
>
> But Homeboy Industries came to Jennifer's assistance, helping her to find a transitional housing program. Able now to pay her rent, Jennifer has started college, and was also able to spend this past Christmas with her children. Not only have the community and support—her new home at Homeboy—given Jennifer this second chance at life, but also she says the love that she finds in and from her new, second family "actually gives me a lot of hope."

**What situations in the world do you think are hopeless? Explain.**

**Have you ever been in a situation that seemed like it was hopeless? Explain.**

## *Hope in the Bible (10 minutes)*

**Materials:** a Bible or this book

Have someone read aloud these verses from Psalm 10, either from a Bible or from this book.

*The Lord rules forever and always!*
*The nations will vanish from his land.*

*Lord, you listen to the desires of those who suffer.*
*You steady their hearts;*
*you listen closely to them,*
*to establish justice*
*for the orphan and the oppressed.*
*Psalm 10:16-18a*

**What do these words say to you about the hope God promises?**

**To whom is God promising hope?**

**How do you think God accomplishes these promises?**

## *More Hope in the Bible (15 minutes)*

**Materials:** Bibles for each group, paper, pens or pencils

We use the word *hope* in a number of different ways. Often we "hope" for things that we want, but are not real or attainable. We say things like, "Don't get your hopes up"; "Don't reach too high because you might fall"; or "Beware of false hopes." Hope defined this way is nothing more than a fanciful wish or dream. But let's look at how the Bible uses the word *hope.*

Divide the class into groups of three or four participants. Assign each group one of the passages below. Have each group rewrite the passage in their own words.

- Ephesians 4:1-4
- Romans 15:1-4
- Isaiah 40:30-31
- Romans 12:9-12
- Jeremiah 29:11-14
- Romans 8:22-26
- Hebrews 11:1-2

> *Therefore, as a prisoner for the Lord, I encourage you to live as people worthy of the call you received from God. Conduct yourselves with all humility, gentleness, and patience. Accept each other with love, and make an effort to preserve the unity of the Spirit with the peace that ties you together. You are one body and one spirit, just as God also called you in one hope.*
>
> *Ephesians 4:1-4*

*We who are powerful need to be patient with the weakness of those who don't have power, and not please ourselves. Each of us should please our neighbors for their good in order to build them up. Christ didn't please himself, but, as it is written,* The insults of those who insulted you fell on me. *Whatever was written in the past was written for our instruction so that we could have hope through endurance and through the encouragement of the scriptures.*

*Romans 15:1-4*

*Youths will become tired and weary,*
*young men will certainly stumble;*
*but those who hope in the Lord*
*will renew their strength;*
*they will fly up on wings like eagles;*
*they will run and not be tired;*
*they will walk and not be weary.*
*Isaiah 40:30-31*

*Love should be shown without pretending. Hate evil, and hold on to what is good. Love each other like the members of your family. Be the best at showing honor to each other. Don't hesitate to be enthusiastic—be on fire in the Spirit as you serve the Lord! Be happy in your hope, stand your ground when you're in trouble, and devote yourselves to prayer.*

*Romans 12:9-12*

*I know the plans I have in mind for you, declares the Lord; they are plans for peace, not disaster, to give you a future filled with hope. When you call me and come and pray to me, I will listen to you. When you search for me, yes, search for me with all your heart, you will find me. I will be present for you, declares the Lord, and I will end your captivity. I will gather you from all the nations and places where I have scattered you, and I will bring you home after your long exile, declares the LORD.*

*Jeremiah 29:11-14*

*We know that the whole creation is groaning together and suffering labor pains up until now. And it's not only the creation. We ourselves who have the Spirit as the first crop of the harvest also groan inside as we wait to be adopted and for our bodies to be set free. We were saved in hope. If we see what we hope for, that isn't hope. Who hopes for what they already see? But if we hope for what we don't see, we wait for it with patience.*

*In the same way, the Spirit comes to help our weakness. We don't know what we should pray, but the Spirit himself pleads our case with unexpressed groans.*

*Romans 8:22-26*

*Faith is the reality of what we hope for, the proof of what we don't see. The elders in the past were approved because they showed faith.*

*Hebrews 11:1-2*

Have a spokesperson from each group read their paraphrase. After each group reads, ask the class:

**Do these passages reflect "false hopes"? Why or why not?**

**When have you hoped in this way?**

After all groups have presented, ask the class:

**Describe a time your hope was disappointed. What do you think went wrong?**

**When has God come through with something you hoped for?**

## *Advent Hopes (10 minutes)*

**Materials:** bowl of papers from the "What If?" activity, large sheet of paper or markerboard, marker

Return to the bowl containing the Christmas if-then statements. Invite volunteers to each pick a paper out of the bowl and read the three hopes written on it. Continue until all the papers have been read. Have someone write all the responses on posted paper or a board where all participants can see them. Ask if anyone wants to add to the list.

**Are these hopes any different from the hopes you hold at other times of the year?**

**What can you do to prepare for the Advent season you hope for?**

**What are you doing in your own community to support the hopes of others? What are you doing outside of your community?**

Read this statement found in Coleman's book *Home for Christmas*:

> As another Christmas draws near, Jennifer knows that being able to spend it with her kids isn't the only thing she has—she also has an entire loving, supportive community holding her up at every time of the year, offering her new life and an always-new creation.

## Closing Prayer

*God, as we approach Christmas, we give thanks for the people who hold us up. Help us be the kinds of people who offer the support and love that will let hope be born and grow. Amen.*

Week 2

# A Home for Love

Unfortunately, I don't remember many specific Christmas seasons. I don't remember many specific church services, Christmas parties, shopping excursions, or holiday concerts. I don't remember many Christmas mornings.

But I remember one. It was my first year of college. I had gone away for school, and was fortunate enough to come home for Christmas. It was a great time to see old friends, to be with my family, to visit my old church, and even to sing again in the church choir. There wasn't much material stuff that I was thinking about, but I was hoping my parents would be able to buy me a camera for Christmas. There were no smartphones then, and I wanted to document my college experience. Christmas Day came, and after I opened a few small gifts, which did not disappoint me, my parents said, "We have one more thing for you." "Let it be a camera, let it be a camera," I thought. The box was too big for a camera, but you know that trick about wrapping smaller gifts in big boxes. I opened the box. It was a television. Apparently, I had talked so much about the television that my roommate had in our tiny room that my parents, who knew I would be moving to another room, thought a television was what I wanted. I wasn't sure how to respond. I felt loved that my parents were trying to read my mind, and I felt unloved because they read wrong. I said, "Thank you." And Dad said, "You don't look very happy." I thanked them for the gift and tried to explain the expression on my face. My loving parents were understanding, and we returned the TV for a camera.

The gift of my parents' love (even when it doesn't deliver what I hoped it would) is, well, a precious gift. And too many people are not as fortunate as I am.

In the Bible, we learn a lot about love from Jonathan; his father, Saul; and Jonathan's son Mephibosheth. Maybe you have heard about Mephibosheth, maybe you haven't. Some would say he had a good life...at least in the beginning. His grandfather, Saul, had been king. And although his dad never got to be king, his dad was lifelong best friends with his dad's successor, King David.

Mephibosheth's dad was Jonathan, and the Bible talks a lot about Jonathan and David's friendship. They made vows to each other when they were young; 1 Samuel says that "Jonathan loved David as much as himself" (1 Samuel 18:3).

Jonathan proved that love over and over. According to the Bible, Jonathan's dad was so jealous of David that he was continually trying to kill David. Jonathan first started warning David, then started hiding him, and then started hiding with him. Jonathan was in such a risky situation that his dad even tried to kill HIM. So as Jonathan showed his love for his friend, David, he was also living through the lack of love from his own father.

Eventually both Jonathan and his dad were killed in a battle. By that time Jonathan had children of his own. His son Mephibosheth was 5 years old when his father and grandfather were killed. After David became king, it was his turn to prove that he understood how to love. He remembered his vow to Jonathan. He wanted that vow to continue to the next generation, so he invited the young Mephibosheth to live in his home. They became family even though they were not blood. They were kin.

Father Boyle likes to talk about radical kinship. At Homeboy, they practice that kinship every day. Person after person talks about the love they have found in their Homeboy family. Truth be told, many had already experienced a kind of family in their gangs. But unlike Jonathan, who would die for his "homie," the gangbangers were more likely to kill for the gang. At Homeboy, they are practicing the power of love.

In some ways, the holiday season is the worst time to think about love. Too often we measure love by material things we hope to be given or by whether certain people have remembered us. That one Christmas Day that I remember left me confused about my parents' love. It shouldn't have. They had showed it in so many ways, even in their attempt to give me the perfect gift.

I have since learned a lot about love. Maybe not enough. But enough to focus more on my loving than my being loved. This is what King David did. After his best friend died, his question was, "Is there anyone left in Jonathan's family that I can show kindness to? How can I demonstrate my continued love for my friend? And how can I make a difference in someone's life?"

At Homeboy, old rivalries die, as people practice kinship—as they work together, pray together, learn together, and laugh together. They bear one another's burdens. And they experience love when they share love.

# ACTIVITIES

Choose from the following activities to form your session.

## *Morning Meeting (5 minutes)*

When I teach in Christian settings, I like to begin each class time with the following recitation: "Hear O Israel. The Lord our God, the Lord is One. Love the Lord your God with all your heart and with all your soul and with all your strength and with all your mind. Love your neighbor as yourself. Do this and you will live."

The recitation is actually a mashup of Luke 10:27-28 and Mark 12:29-31. In Luke, Jesus is asked what people should do to attain eternal life. In Mark, Jesus is asked what the greatest commandment is. In both cases Jesus affirms these basic words: "Love God and love your neighbor."

The message was echoed at the wedding of Prince Harry of the United Kingdom and American actress and humanitarian Meghan Markle, now the Duke and Duchess of Sussex. I admit to not being very attentive to the British royal family. But this wedding caught my attention, especially the sermon delivered by Bishop Michael Curry of the American Episcopal Church. Bishop Curry spoke about the power of love. He said,

> Oh, there's power—power in love. Not just in its romantic forms, but any form, any shape of love. There's a certain sense in which when you are loved, and you know it, when someone cares for you, and you know it, when you love and you show it—it actually feels right. There's something right about it.
>
> And there's a reason for it. The reason has to do with the source. We were made by a power of love, and our lives were meant—and are meant—to be lived in that love. That's why we are here.[1]

Sometimes it's difficult to know what is most important in our Christian lives. After years of reading the Bible and other Christian literature, I have decided to filter all new spiritual teachings through those words. It matters to me that, for Jesus, the Greatest Commandment is also the key to life. And according to Jesus, love is that key.

1 Michael Curry, "'The Power of Love'—Bishop Michael Curry's Sermon at the Wedding of Prince Harry and Meghan Markle," sermon, St. George's Chapel at Windsor Castle, Windsor, England, May 19, 2018, The Archbishop of Canterbury website, https://www.archbishopofcanterbury.org/speaking-and-writing/sermons/power-love-bishop-michael-currys-sermon-wedding-prince-harry-and.

## *Do You Love Your Neighbor? (7–10 minutes)*

**Materials:** chairs

Have participants sit in a circle of chairs. Have one person stand in the center of the circle. To start the game, the center person walks up to someone in the chairs and asks, "Do you love your neighbor?"

The response can be something like "Yes, especially people with black hair," or "Yes, especially people who are wearing red." At that point everyone with black hair (or wearing red) gets up and changes seats. The center person tries to take one of the seats as well, leaving a new center person.

The response to the question can also be "No." In that case, the two people on either side of the responder have to get up and switch seats. The center person tries to take one of their seats.

After a few rounds of the game, begin the love discussion in the next activity.

## *From the Bible (15–20 minutes)*

**Materials:** Bibles or this book, paper, pens or pencils

Remind participants that the idea of loving our neighbors is found in Luke 10, the story that we call the Good Samaritan. Have participants read the story either in Bibles or from the text below. Then have participants work in groups of three to six people. Each group should retell the story in one of the modern-day settings and groups listed here either by acting it out or by simply rewriting it.

After the presentations, ask:

**What does this story teach us about love?**

**Is this love a feeling, words, or actions?**

The settings/groups:

- A modern-day church
- A film company
- A hospital
- A university
- A grade school
- An IT company
- A sports team

The story:

> *A legal expert stood up to test Jesus. "Teacher," he said, "what must I do to gain eternal life?"*
>
> *Jesus replied, "What is written in the Law? How do you interpret it?"*
>
> *He responded,* "You must love the Lord your God with all your heart, with all your being, with all your strength, and with all your mind, and love your neighbor as yourself."
>
> *Jesus said to him, "You have answered correctly. Do this and you will live."*
>
> *But the legal expert wanted to prove that he was right, so he said to Jesus, "And who is my neighbor?"*
>
> *Jesus replied, "A man went down from Jerusalem to Jericho. He encountered thieves, who stripped him naked, beat him up, and left him near death. Now it just so happened that a priest was*

*also going down the same road. When he saw the injured man, he crossed over to the other side of the road and went on his way. Likewise, a Levite came by that spot, saw the injured man, and crossed over to the other side of the road and went on his way. A Samaritan, who was on a journey, came to where the man was. But when he saw him, he was moved with compassion. The Samaritan went to him and bandaged his wounds, tending them with oil and wine. Then he placed the wounded man on his own donkey, took him to an inn, and took care of him. The next day, he took two full days' worth of wages and gave them to the innkeeper. He said, 'Take care of him, and when I return, I will pay you back for any additional costs.' What do you think? Which one of these three was a neighbor to the man who encountered thieves?"*

*Then the legal expert said, "The one who demonstrated mercy toward him."*

*Jesus told him, "Go and do likewise."*

*Luke 10:25-37*

## Brainstorm Love Songs (5–7 minutes)

**Materials:** large sheet of paper or markerboard, marker

Ask students to call out names of popular love songs. Record these songs on posted paper or a board.

**What do these songs say about love?**

**How are these songs like or unlike the love in the story of the Good Samaritan?**

**What other kinds of love are there?**

## *Tell Carl's Story (10 minutes)*

At Homeboy Ministries Carl found a love that makes a difference. As Justin Coleman writes,

> Carl admits that the atmosphere at Homeboy Industries might be a little disorienting to visitors, who are probably used to seeing tattoos and thinking, "Gangs! Danger!" Visitors may expect the homeboys and homegirls to give them "some type of look" demanding to know why they're there—may expect anything but the loving welcome they receive when they walk through the doors. Carl says it's the evident kinship at Homeboy that helped him learn how to communicate with other people—and how to love both them and himself. "That's love for me," he says: the fact that this place has brought together onetime enemies and turned them into family.

**How is the love Carl talks about like the love in pop songs?**

**How is it different?**

## *A Loving Home (5–7 minutes)*

**Materials:** large sheet of paper or markerboard, marker

**What are qualities of a loving home?**

Write answers on posted paper or on a board. If participants are reluctant to answer, have them gather first in groups of two to six, then have the groups report to the class.

**How is the love Carl talks about like the love in a loving home?**

**How is it different?**

## *How We Love (10–15 minutes)*

**Materials:** a Bible or this book

Have someone read aloud:

> *Love is patient, love is kind, it isn't jealous, it doesn't brag, it isn't arrogant, it isn't rude, it doesn't seek its own advantage, it isn't*

> *irritable, it doesn't keep a record of complaints, it isn't happy with injustice, but it is happy with the truth. Love puts up with all things, trusts in all things, hopes for all things, endures all things. Love never fails.*
>
> *1 Corinthians 13:4-8a*

Let's return to the settings and groups we spoke of earlier.

- A modern-day church
- A film company
- A hospital
- A university
- A grade school
- An IT company
- A sports team

**If people in these groups practiced this kind of love, what would they do?**

**How would they act?**

**What effect might this kind of loving have on them?**

**What makes this kind of loving difficult?**

**Can you think of a time when someone was judged for his or her problems?**

**What would loving look like in that situation?**

**Do you think acting out of love instead of judgment is especially important as Christians? Why or why not?**

**If acting out of love instead of judgment is especially important as Christians, how do we do so?**

## *Love in My Community (10 minutes)*

**Materials:** a Bible or this book

Have someone read aloud this Philippians 1 passage either from the Bible or from this book.

> *I thank my God every time I mention you in my prayers. I'm thankful for all of you every time I pray, and it's always a prayer*

*full of joy. I'm glad because of the way you have been my partners in the ministry of the gospel from the time you first believed it until now. I'm sure about this: the one who started a good work in you will stay with you to complete the job by the day of Christ Jesus. I have good reason to think this way about all of you because I keep you in my heart. You are all my partners in God's grace, both during my time in prison and in the defense and support of the gospel. God is my witness that I feel affection for all of you with the compassion of Christ Jesus.*

*This is my prayer: that your love might become even more and more rich with knowledge and all kinds of insight. I pray this so that you will be able to decide what really matters and so you will be sincere and blameless on the day of Christ. I pray that you will then be filled with the fruit of righteousness, which comes from Jesus Christ, in order to give glory and praise to God.*

*Philippians 1:3-11*

**Who is your neighbor?**

**What would loving every person in this way look like?**

Have someone read aloud the passage a second time, this time more slowly. Invite participants to imagine a loved one saying these words to them. The loved one could be a mentor, a parent or grandparent, a teacher, a youth leader, a pastor, or a friend.

**How does it feel hearing those words from your loved one?**

**Is there someone you would like to express these kinds of words to?**

## *Affirmations (5–7 minutes)*

**Materials:** paper, pens or pencils

Have participants sit in a circle. Hand out sheets of paper and pencils or pens. Have them all turn to the person on their right and write three things they appreciate about the person. Someone who doesn't know the person on the right well can write three prayers or blessings for the person.

Then have each participant pass the paper to the person on her or his right. Allow any participants who want to to share aloud elements on the paper they received.

Close in prayer.

## Week 3

# A Home for Joy

I'm usually pretty good at finding things that I've lost, but, well, not always. On this one occasion I was feeling tense. There was a churning in my stomach, a restlessness in my bones. And my mind was alternately single-minded and scattered. Why? Because we had bought three avocados in the last few days; they'd been trying to ripen for guacamole. I finally decided they were ripe enough, and I gathered all my stuff. But I could only find two avocados! I *really* wanted three.

I know what happened. "Somebody" (he's about 15 months old) thought the avocado was a "ball" and played "Put It in the Cabinet" or "Put It in the Drawer" or "Throw It Over There." No one was watching him that particular moment, and now somewhere in our house an avocado was rotting.

I know: one out of three avocados shouldn't have that much power in my life. For your information, I don't really think it was the avocados. I think it was Moby's CD *Play* (actually it's the two-CD set). Before I started looking for the avocado, I started looking for the CDs. It was an all-day search. I was actually looking for Moby for a work project. Since I have CDs both at work and home, I looked all day both places. Whenever I didn't have to think about something else, my mind was working on where Moby could be.

I asked the teenagers in our home. They all let me know either by words or tone that they were not really fans of Moby anyway. Not the point.

Maybe it was in that black bag I carried back and forth from work. Maybe it was in that box, or that one, or that one, or the closet I'd already looked in four times. Finally I told my wife, "If it's not in that black bag (wherever *that* is), I give up. I'll have to save my pennies and order another one." I found the black bag. It was not there. I gave up. The churning lessened.

I shifted gears and started cleaning up my ongoing mess in the home office. Too much stuff, I know. I thought cleaning up a little clutter might de-clutter my mind. I decided to empty one last box so I could get rid of it. Just empty this box and I can get rid of it. I thought "There, it's emptied. And what's this behind it? Oh, Moby!" Now if we could only find that rotting avocado.

Even without the avocado (we must have found it eventually), I felt that joy. And the search reminded me of the stories Jesus told about lost things. We mentioned one of those stories two weeks ago, when we focused on the love a father had for his lost son. The story goes on to demonstrate the joy the father had for the return of his son, even though his son had insulted and embarrassed him. The same chapter in the Bible talks about a sheep-gatherer who has lost one sheep, and a poor woman who has lost one coin. Like me, they dropped everything to look for their lost thing. Unlike me they never stopped looking. And then, the boy was home, the sheep was returned, the coin was found. And the searchers were filled with joy!

When we think about joy, we don't always think about those everyday simple joys. We think maybe of celebrations or of something we are anticipating. During the Advent season, joy is often tied to those kinds of pursuits. But there is a deeper kind of joy that is longer lasting.

Father Boyle has seen it in his homegirls and homeboys. Many of them were searching for family, security, and survival. Joy was not on their minds. But in time, joy surprised them.

# ACTIVITIES

Choose from the following activities to form your session.

## *Morning Meeting (5 minutes)*

The woman in front of me at the grocery store just volunteered information to the cashier. "Yes, I'm buying this ice cream. It just looked so good, and I don't even like ice cream!"

That's marketing for you! The most effective marketers or salespeople or product displays can sell us something we don't even want. It works because we are continually in search of something that will bring us joy. We are not always aware of it, until we come home with unwanted ice cream.

Our wanting to feel joy or satisfaction or happiness is not the problem. We are born with the wanting. And in our best circumstances, from birth we learn to find joy in the simplest things.

At a young age, children are sponges, absorbing what we share with them and then sharing it back to us and the world. We smile, they smile. We laugh, they laugh. We pour joy over them and then they mirror that joy.

We don't ever really lose what we first learned. We learn to be selective about what we do or do not receive into our lives. But we still act as sponges. We take things in and then we pour things out into the world.

So many of the personal struggles that we face result from the ways we seek to find joy. Sometimes bad habits help us, as Justin Coleman puts it, "to numb or take the edge off of what we are feeling. We seek to take the edge off of pain through things that bring us instant comfort or gratification.... We take the edge off of our boredom by various kinds of entertainment, sometimes dangerous and unhealthy ones." But we take the edge off of joy when we just numb ourselves.

Homegirls and homeboys like Theo, whose story we will hear, have learned to open themselves to life, beyond the numbing. They have found ways to find lasting joy, even when their lives are difficult.

## *Tell Theo's Story (5–7 minutes)*

Read the following passage found in *Home for Christmas*:

> Before he got involved with Homeboy Industries, Theo felt trapped in a negative environment. Using drugs, spending most of his time in the street with gang members, he says he was "heartbroken." But as Father Gregory Boyle and the staff at Homeboy began offering him support and assistance, Theo says he began "opening up his eyes." He was astounded that people from outside his neighborhood were willing not only to welcome and help him but also to provide more support than any people he'd known before. In this place where the doors are never closed to anyone, Theo experiences "a feeling of joy" being around onetime enemies who now "are just a single family"—who, he says, "look out for one another."

**What does Theo's story tell us about finding joy?**

**What is the source of his joy?**

**How does he pursue joy?**

## *Jesus Joy (10–15 minutes)*

**Materials:** a Bible or this book, paper, pens or pencils

Theo is actually echoing some of Jesus' teachings. As recorded in the book of Matthew, Jesus once sat in front of a large group of followers and talked about the things that can bring joy, that can make us "happy."

Have someone read aloud this passage in Matthew from a Bible or from this book:

> *Now when Jesus saw the crowds, he went up a mountain. He sat down and his disciples came to him. He taught them, saying:*
>
> *"Happy are people who are hopeless, because the kingdom of heaven is theirs.*
>
> *"Happy are people who grieve, because they will be made glad.*
>
> *"Happy are people who are humble, because they will inherit the earth.*
>
> *"Happy are people who are hungry and thirsty for righteousness, because they will be fed until they are full.*
>
> *"Happy are people who show mercy, because they will receive mercy.*
>
> *"Happy are people who have pure hearts, because they will see God.*
>
> *"Happy are people who make peace, because they will be called God's children.*
>
> *"Happy are people whose lives are harassed because they are righteous, because the kingdom of heaven is theirs.*
>
> *"Happy are you when people insult you and harass you and speak all kinds of bad and false things about you, all because of me. Be full of joy and be glad, because you have a great reward in heaven. In the same way, people harassed the prophets who came before you."*
>
> *Matthew 5:1-12*

Have participants gather in groups of four to six people. Have each group identify someone, known publicly or personally, who exemplifies each of the "Happy Statements." Have each group take two or three of the statements. They should identify:

- Person's name
- Why they chose that person
- How the person exemplifies the "Happy Statement"

Allow time for groups to report back. Then ask,

**How are these statements like happiness in Theo's story?**

**How are these statements not like happiness in Theo's story?**

## *Advertisement Search (10 minutes)*

**Materials:** paper, pens or pencils

In our everyday lives, some of us we aren't dealing with persecution or poverty. What does joy in any circumstance look like for us? Marketers and advertisers are hoping they know. They like to figure out what will make us feel joy and then they want to sell it to us. Let's look at how they do so.

Divide participants into groups of four to six people. Assign one of the products on the following page to each group (or allow a group to suggest another product with your approval). Each group should think about television, radio, online, or print advertisements for the product, and answer.

**What are they selling?**

**Describe one commercial or sing/recite one catch phrase.**

**What are they promising?**

**What want are they wanting to fill?**

- KitKat
- GEICO
- Gatorade
- Hardee's/Carl's Jr.
- Barbie
- Subaru
- Avengers trailer
- Aleve
- MyPillow
- TRESemmé
- Carnival Cruise Line
- Pepsi

Have groups report back to the whole class. Then ask,

**According to these ads, what is the key to joy?**

**How is this like or unlike other messages about joy?**

## *Everyday Joy (5–7 minutes)*

**Materials:** a Bible or this book

Read the following passage found in *Home for Christmas*:

> The concept of joy has a whole history in the Scriptures, and is, of course, deeply connected to God and God's very nature. Often, it seems that Scripture is telling us that joy is something God has, something that we need to be given. For example, joy is mentioned in Ecclesiastes 5:18-20 as something that is given to humankind by God as a gift.

Have someone read the Scripture passage aloud.

> *This is the one good thing I've seen: it's appropriate for people to eat, drink, and find enjoyment in all their hard work under the sun during the brief lifetime that God gives them because that's their lot in life. Also, whenever God gives people wealth and riches and enables them to enjoy it, to accept their place in the world and to find pleasure in their hard work—all this is God's gift. Indeed, people shouldn't brood too much over the days of their lives because God gives an answer in their hearts' joy.*
>
> *Ecclesiastes 5:18-20*

**Is there any special way in which the Christmas season is joyful for you?**

**What makes it unlike the joy you find during other times of the year?**

## *These Bring Me Joy (10 minutes)*

**Materials:** paper and writing utensil for each participant

Hand out a sheet of paper and pen or pencil to each person. Have them number the paper 1–10, leaving at least enough space to write down three words per number. If the paper is lined, have participants leave two lines after each number.

Then read off each of these partial sentences. After each sentence, allow time for participants to write responses.

If time permits after all of the answers are written, invite participants to tell the group some of their answers.

- I'm thankful for these three things I hear:
- I'm thankful for these three things I see:
- I'm thankful for these three things I smell:
- I'm thankful for these three things I touch/feel:
- I'm thankful for these three things I taste:
- I'm thankful for these three holiday things:

- I'm thankful for these three friends:
- I'm thankful for these three teachers:
- I'm thankful for these three family members:
- I'm thankful for these three things in my home:

**How did this exercise feel?**

**Did any of anyone's answers surprise you?**

**Did any of your own answers surprise you?**

## *Joy in Scripture (5–7 minutes)*

**Materials:** a Bible or this book

Have someone read aloud these verses from Philippians.

> *Be glad in the Lord always! Again I say, be glad! Let your gentleness show in your treatment of all people. The Lord is near. Don't be anxious about anything; rather, bring up all of your requests to God in your prayers and petitions, along with giving thanks. Then the peace of God that exceeds all understanding will keep your hearts and minds safe in Christ Jesus.*
>
> *Philippians 4:4-7*

**What does it mean to be glad in the Lord?**

**How do we do so actively?**

Reread this passage as a closing prayer.

## Week 4

# A Home for Peace

So I am officially part of the genealogy craze. Well, sort of. A friend who is into those searches volunteered to do some work for my wife, who is trying to find a lost sister. The friend offered to pay to have both my DNA and my wife's tested, through one of the popular ancestry search companies. We were surprised by some of the results, namely that I don't have the Native American ancestry that I'd always been told I have.

It's all a craze now, but genealogies are nothing new. Even without the Internet, databases, and DNA, folks have been documenting and researching genealogies throughout human history.

In the Bible, the Book of Numbers is largely about counting people and documenting who came from whom. Throughout the books of 1 and 2 Samuel, 1 and 2 Kings, and 1 and 2 Chronicles we learn about the same things: Who was the father of whom? And then the books of Matthew and Luke trace the ancestry of Jesus of Nazareth. In ancient Palestine, that practice mainly involved tracing the men, not women, in someone's line. But Matthew adds four women. And to some readers, these four are unusual choices.

Tamar is in the line. Tamar was the twice-widowed and once-jilted Canaanite woman who ended up sleeping with her father-in-law and producing children. Tamar is a great-grandmother of Jesus.

Rahab is in the line. Rahab is known for harboring spies and lying about it. Rahab is later mentioned as an example of faith and obedience. Rahab is a great-grandmother of Jesus.

Bathsheba is in the line. Bathsheba is known not so much for what she did, but for what others did. King David saw her one day, sent for her, seduced her, and then had her husband killed so that he could have Bathsheba for himself. Bathsheba is the mother of King Solomon and a great-grandmother of Jesus.

And Ruth is in the line. Let's spend some more time talking about Ruth and Naomi.

The story of Ruth and Naomi is the story of home on the run. Like me and my family, Ruth could not define "home" by a building or even a place. Her circumstances wouldn't let her. Here's what happened as recorded in the Bible book of Ruth, which could just as easily be called The Book of Naomi:

Naomi was from Bethlehem, the same town that Jesus would be born in centuries later. Naomi was married to Elimelech. When a famine hit Bethlehem and the surrounding areas, Naomi, Elimelech, and their two sons set out as refugees in Moab. The Moabites were not always friendly to the Israelites. There was history. But Naomi, Elimelech, and their sons settled there to escape that famine.

We don't know how long they lived in Moab before Elimelech died. But we know that when he died his sons took Moabite wives, Orpah and Ruth. Then the sons died, leaving Naomi, Orpah, and Ruth all as widows. Naomi decided to go home to Bethlehem, and she wisely suggested—really ordered—her daughters-in-law to go back to their homes, each to their "mother's house." It made sense in their culture. As Naomi explained it, in essence, "You can go back home, and you are young enough to find a new husband." Orpah thought that made sense, but Ruth did not agree. She argued with her mother-in-law, and eventually said now-famous words: "Wherever you go, I will go; and wherever you stay, I will stay. Your people will be my people, and your God will be my God" (Ruth 1:16).

She was saying, "My home is not where I come from, my home is not where I currently reside, my home is with my loved ones. And right now, Naomi, my home is with you."

The homeboys and homegirls of Homeboy Industries can share that sentiment. Father Gregory Boyle likes to talk about "the power of radical kinship." At times, former gang enemies have banded together and bonded into a family.

# ACTIVITIES

Choose from the following activities to form your session.

## *Morning Meeting (5 minutes)*

I Googled it. It turns out there actually is a list of the most memorable fights in Christmas movies. I was looking for one in particular, but I stumbled upon a bunch. *Elf* has a fight. So do *A Christmas Story*, *Scrooged*, *Home Alone*, and *Christmas with the Kranks*. Even a classic black-and-white film like *It's a Wonderful Life* features a fight scene. But the scene I was looking for shows up in 1996's *Jingle All the Way*. In this movie, two rival fathers, workaholic Howard Langston (Arnold Schwarzenegger) and stressed-out postal worker Myron Larabee (Sinbad), both want to get a Turbo-Man action figure for their respective sons. It's Christmas Eve, and both men are on a last-minute shopping spree. When you Google "Jingle All the Way fight scene," what comes up first is a pretty violent scene when Schwarzenegger's character gets into a brawl with a bunch of Santas. The whole movie is fueled by the pressures of the holiday season. And it sounds familiar to us because so much of the season can be full of tension. Some of the tension can be avoided, for instance by taking away the emphasis on getting things or by limiting the number of activities that have to fit into the season.

But other tensions are just there. They come from relationships broken or strained, from bad memories, or from hard-to-let-go-of expectations.

It might sound a little strange that we emphasize the peace of the season just as those tensions are the hottest.

For many folks at Homeboy Industries, the seasonal conflict might be heightened by a history that has had no peace. The sweet peaceful home pictures that many portray around this time do not reflect the reality of these homegirls and homeboys. They have memories of anything but peace. There are memories of gang warfare, of insecure homes, of unstable relationships. Add those memories to the stress of the season, and the mixture can be volatile.

But at Homeboy, many have come to embrace peace. Some rival gangbangers have become best friends. Many from difficult homes have found family and home. Some who were away from their family members have been reunited.

For all of us, it is tempting to get caught up in the tensions and forget the season. But in every week of this season, on every day, in every moment, we can decide to embrace the peace as we anticipate the coming of the Prince of Peace.

## *Silent Grouping (7–10 minutes)*

This activity involves the whole class, and the directions are simple. In each round, participants are to group themselves by a certain criterion. However, participants must accomplish the task without speaking.

- Round 1: Group by birth month
- Round 2: Group by birth year (age)

**What happened during the game?**

**What skills did we use during the game?**

**How was it to communicate without speaking?**

**What worked?**

## *Tell Christina's Story (5–7 minutes)*

Read the following passage found in Justin Coleman's *Home for Christmas*:

> Before Christina came to Homeboy Industries, she was having a hard time on her own—with the big things, like getting sober and finishing school, and even with the things that should have been easy, like spending time with her daughter. But Homeboy has been helping to make things less stressful for her, providing Christina with tools to help her focus, to form relationships, to live the life she wants to live. One of the things she values about the therapy sessions and the classes Homeboy offers her is the fact that, as she says, "everyone is going through the exact same thing you are going through. It feels so good to have that support." She credits the organization with helping her work toward her high school diploma, and toward becoming a drug and alcohol counselor. And even more importantly, Homeboy has given her the peace "to be present" with her daughter. Because of this loving home of strangers who have become

a family, Christina has also found the peace that has enabled her to make a new, loving home with the family she's always had.

Say, "Don't we all want to find that peace in our homes and families? Christmas is around the corner as we anticipate the arrival of our Prince of Peace. But the closer we get to that day, most of us feel anything but peaceful."

**What are some of the more stressful parts of the holidays?**

**What expectations cause stress?**

**What activities cause stress?**

## *Grouping, Part Two (7–10 minutes)*

Play a third and fourth round, with the same directions as above: in each round, participants are to group themselves by a certain criterion. However, participants must accomplish the task without speaking. Choose from the categories below, or create your own similar categories.

- School you attend
- Favorite sports team
- Favorite recent movie
- Favorite musical style

**Have you ever had a heated conversation with someone who disagreed with you on one of these things?**

**If so, how did the conversation escalate?**

**Was the conflict resolved? If not, why not? If so, how?**

## *Sharing Joy (7 minutes)*

**Materials:** a Bible or this book

Christmas movies, especially comedies, like to make light of holiday stress. A lot of them highlight stresses in relationships, even with people we don't know. The Bible has something to say about those relationships.

Have someone read aloud these verses from Romans:

> *Bless people who harass you—bless and don't curse them. Be happy with those who are happy, and cry with those who are crying. Consider everyone as equal, and don't think that you're better than anyone else. Instead, associate with people who have no status. Don't think that you're so smart. Don't pay back anyone for their evil actions with evil actions, but show respect for what everyone else believes is good.*
>
> *If possible, to the best of your ability, live at peace with all people.*
>
> *Romans 12:14-18*

**On a scale of 1 to 10, how hard is it to "bless people who harass you"? To pay back evil actions with good?**

**On a scale of 1 to 10, how hard is it to "be happy with those who are happy"? To "cry with those who are crying"?**

**On a scale of 1 to 10, how hard is it to "consider everyone as equal"? To "associate with people who have no status"?**

**On a scale of 1 to 10, how hard is it to "live at peace with all people"?**

## *Becoming Peace-Loving (10 minutes)*

**Materials:** a Bible or this book

Have someone read aloud these verses from Psalm 37:

*The mouths of the righteous recite wisdom;*
*their tongues discuss justice.*

*The Instruction of their God is in their hearts;*
*they don't miss a step.*
*The wicked, on the other hand, target the righteous,*
*seeking to kill them.*
*But the Lord won't leave the righteous*
*to the power of the wicked,*
*and won't let the righteous*
*be found guilty when they are judged.*

*Hope in the Lord and keep his way!*
*He will lift you up so you can possess the land.*
*When the wicked are eliminated,*
*you will see it for yourself!*
*I myself have seen wicked powerful people,*
*exalting themselves like a stately cedar.*
*But when I came back, they were gone!*
*I looked all over for them,*
*but they couldn't be found!*

*Observe those who have integrity*
*and watch those whose heart is right*
*because the future belongs to persons of peace.*

*Psalm 37:30-37*

**Do you agree that the world can be divided into wicked people and peace-loving people?**

**Can a person change from a peace-loving to a wicked person? If not, why not? If so, how?**

**Can a person change from a wicked to a peace-loving person? If not, why not? If so, how?**

## *Stress/Destress (10 minutes)*

**Materials:** a Bible or this book, two uninflated balloons, and a few more for backup

Hold one balloon and inflate it about halfway.

Say something like, "Sometimes holiday tension comes into our lives, and that tension builds as we give time, energy, and thinking to dealing with problems. We have some options at this time. We can keep focusing on only the problems, and they often get bigger and bigger."

Begin blowing more air into the balloon.

Say, "The more we worry, the more stress is added." Keep blowing until the balloon pops.

**What are some of those tensions and difficulties?**

**What does our frustration look like?**

**What are some unhelpful ways to deal with the difficulties?**

Take another balloon and blow it up about halfway.

Say, "But we do have options. There are actions we can take. We can slow down, we can talk to a trusted friend or family member, we can pray. As we begin to take these actions, our tension can ease."

Let some air out of the balloon.

**Have you tried these actions to ease tension?**

**Have they been effective? Why or why not?**

**What other actions have been effective for you?**

Read John 16:33:

> *"I've said these things to you so that you will have peace in me. In the world you have distress. But be encouraged! I have conquered the world."*

Let the balloon go so that it flies round the room until it's deflated.

## *Bringing It Back Home*

**Materials:** a Bible or this book

The peace of Christ that grounds Homeboy Industries allows people like Christina to see good in places where it seemed impossible. It's what we see happening in Ephesians 2. Have someone read the passage aloud:

> *Christ is our peace. He made both Jews and Gentiles into one group. With his body, he broke down the barrier of hatred that divided us. He canceled the detailed rules of the Law so that he could create one new person out of the two groups, making peace. He reconciled them both as one body to God by the cross, which ended the hostility to God.*
>
> *When he came, he announced the good news of peace to you who were far away from God and to those who were near.*
>
> *Ephesians 2:14-17*

# Notes

CPSIA information can be obtained
at www.ICGtesting.com
Printed in the USA
LVHW05s0114250718
584811LV00004B/5/P

9 781501 870422